THE WORLD OF

English

Revision

Alison Head

Contents

Two is Too Many!

Isabella Witherbottom was horrified to find not one but two large, hairy spiders hiding under her bed.

"Max!" she yelled. "Spiders! Come quickly!"

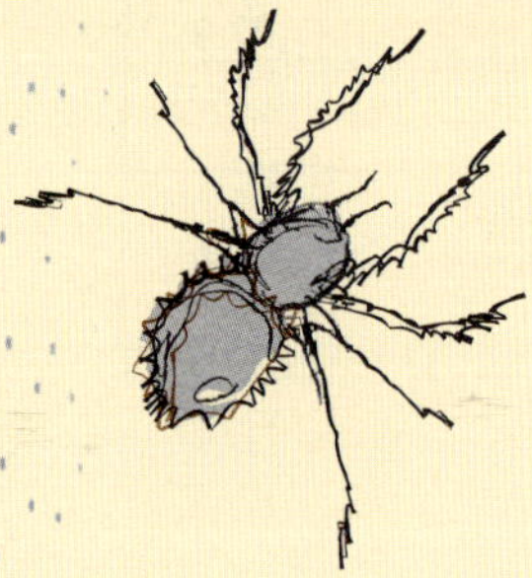

"Calm down, Izzy," said Max, the butler. "A couple of spiders are nothing to worry about. In fact, most **plurals** are easy to deal with if you don't panic. Plural just means more than one, and with most plural **nouns** you can just add *s*. Like with *spiders*, Izzy," said Max with a chuckle.

"On the other hand," he went on, "some nouns end in a hissing or buzzing type of sound, like *bus*, or *watch*, and with those you add *es* to make them plural, so you would write *buses* or *watches*."

"Well that sounds much easier than dealing with spiders. Is that really all I need to know?" asked Isabella.

"Not quite," replied Max. "You need to know what happens to words that end in *y*. If the word ends in a **vowel** and then *y*, like *trolley*, you can just add *s*, to make *trolleys*. But, if it ends in a **consonant** then *y*, like *lady*, you have to take off the *y*, and add *ies*, so you would write *ladies*.

"Then of course there are a few words which don't follow the rules and change completely when they become plurals, like *mouse* and *mice*. You'll just have to learn those separately, I'm afraid," he went on.

Isabella shuddered. "Yuk, mice. They give me the creeps too!"

Say what you see

Look at all the junk under this bed. Write a list of all the things lurking under there, saying how many of each thing you can see. Take care to spell the plurals correctly.

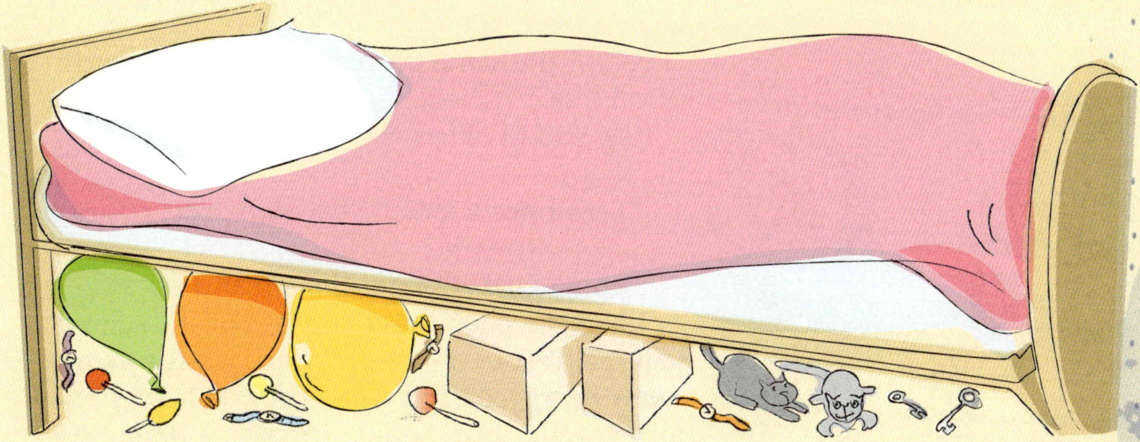

Top Tips

To help you remember to add *es* to words ending in a hissing or buzzing sound, try saying them out loud – you can hear the extra syllable clearly.

Did you know?

Some words don't have a **singular** form at all, for instance *trousers, scissors* and *spectacles.* Other words have no plural form, for instance *sheep, bison* and *deer.*

Can You Believe Your Eyes?

Sir Ralph Witherbottom was trying to identify an unusual bird in a tree in the garden.

"It looks like a purple-throated warbler, but it doesn't sound like one. Most curious," he remarked.

"I've got the same problem with these words, Dad," said Isabella. "They all look similar, but they sound different."

"Let's have a look," said Sir Ralph.

"Look, Dad. *Plough*, *though* and *enough* all have the *ough* letter string, but it makes a different sound in each word. It's the same with *bear*, *year* and *earn*. They all have the *ear* letter string, but, again, it makes a different sound in each word," complained Isabella.

"Yes, Izzy," sympathised Sir Ralph. "Those words can be tricky. You see, you can't always be sure that words with similar spellings will be **pronounced** the same. Thankfully, we use most of these words quite a lot, so reading them isn't usually a problem. It's spelling them that can be tough. Thankfully, you can sometimes get a clue from the other letters in the word. So an *e* before the letter string *ight* will usually make a long *ay* sound, like in *eight*. Otherwise, *ight* tends to give an *eye* sound, like in *light*, or *fright*."

"Oh dear!" groaned Isabella. "Sounds like hard work!"

"Well the best thing about these tricky words is that there really aren't very many of them, so you can learn them all in no time. And don't forget – you can always check your spelling in a dictionary if you want to be sure. Which reminds me, have you seen my bird book?" asked Sir Ralph.

Sort the sounds

This tree is full of the different sounds made by unpredictable letter strings. Can you add words from the box to the end of each branch?

- bright
- learn
- fried
- shield
- gear
- bough
- wear
- though
- weight
- enough

Top Tips!

If you find some of these words particularly confusing, try using a **mnemonic** to help you remember how to spell them. Mnemonics are memorable phrases you can use to help you remember tricky spellings. For example, big ears and ugly teeth yuk! can help you to spell *beauty*.

Did you know?

How these different words strings are pronounced will often depend on your accent. So spelling tricks that work for one person might not for someone else.

Suffix Style

Isabella Witherbottom was getting ready to go out, but just couldn't decide what to wear.

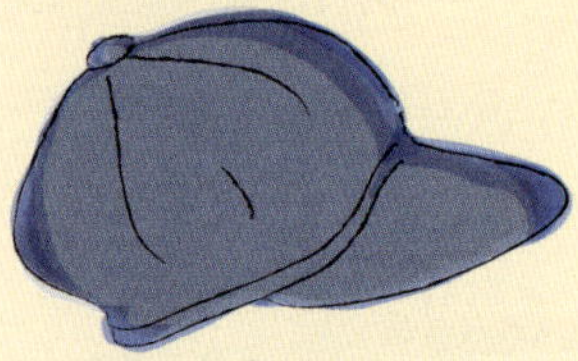

"What do you think, Max?" she asked. "Hat, or no hat? I can't decide on anything today. I couldn't do my homework either, because I couldn't decide whether to keep the *e* or take it off when I was adding **suffixes**."

"Well, I'm no good with fashion," said Max, the butler, "but I'm sure I can help with those suffixes. And you're certainly not going out till you've done your homework anyway, so why don't you tell me what you're supposed to do."

"OK, OK! We have to add suffixes to words ending in *e*. I know you have to take off the *e* sometimes, but I can't decide when to take it off and when to leave it," said Isabella.

"That's simple, Izzy," replied Max. "It all depends on the suffix. If you are adding a **vowel** suffix to a word ending in *e*, you have to take the *e* off first. Vowel suffixes include *ing, ed, ish, est, ism, er, al* and *able*. So the word *take* becomes *taking* not *takeing*, and *spoke* becomes *spoken*, not *spokeen*."

"I see, Max. So *rehearse* becomes *rehearsal* and *love* becomes *lovable*. But what about **consonant** suffixes?" asked Isabella.

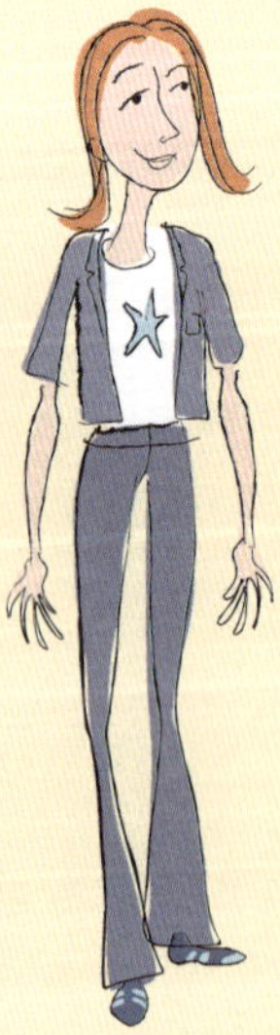

"With those, you keep the *e*," explained Max. "Consonant suffixes are *ful, ment, less, ness* and *ly*. So you would write *nicely*, and *pavement*, rather than *nicly* and *pavment*."

"Brilliant. That's suffixes taken care of," said Isabella. "Now, what about this hat?"

4 Write down the plural form of these singular nouns.

a dish ____________________

b patch ____________________

c ball ____________________

d city ____________________

e house ____________________

f child ____________________

5 Find two words from the box that contain each of these letter strings.

heard bright height relief tie near

a ear ____________ ____________

b ie ____________ ____________

c ight ____________ ____________

6 Underline the suffixes in these words.

a saving

b ageless

c usable

d careful

e sharing

f biggest

The Same but Different

Isabella Witherbottom had been shut in her room working on a story for ages, and Sir Ralph guessed it wasn't going very well.

"What's the matter, Izzy? Having trouble?" he asked.

"I've gone from fed up to cross, to angry, and now I'm furious! I just can't think of the right words and when I do get a good one, I end up having to use it over and over again," wailed Isabella.

"Ah, you need **synonyms**. You're actually rather good at them already, you just don't know it yet," said Sir Ralph.

"How can I be good at them when I don't even know what they are?" asked a confused Isabella.

"Synonyms are words with a similar meaning, like *cross* and *angry*. Using synonyms can save you from having to use the same word again and again," explained Sir Ralph.

"Well I certainly need some of them, then," said Isabella.

"The really clever thing about synonyms, however, is that they usually don't mean exactly the same thing, so you can pick from the range of meanings to help you write precisely what you mean," he went on. "Take what you said to me just now. You started off *fed up*, but by the time I came in you had shot up the scale to *furious*. I knew exactly how you felt, because you had picked the right synonym from the scale."

"So I did. I'm actually rather good at this, aren't I?" exclaimed Isabella. "In fact, I'm brilliant. Fantastic. Amazing!"

Match the meanings

Sort the words in the box into the right order, then use them to label the thermometer.

cold hot chilly freezing tepid cool warm boiling

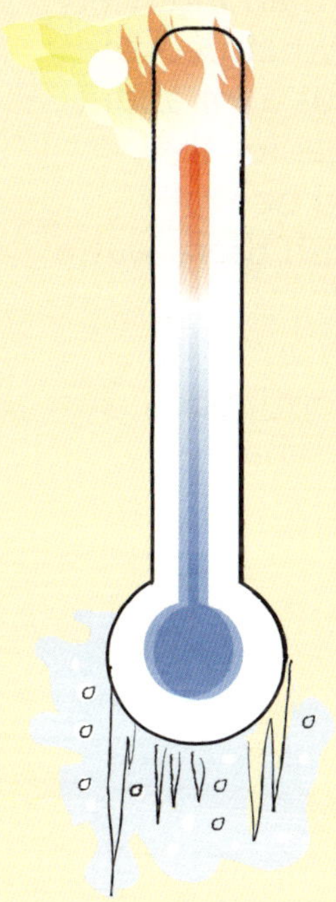

Top Tips!

If you want to be sure you have picked the very best synonym, check exactly what it means by looking it up in the dictionary.

Did you know?

You can find lots of synonyms in a special book called a thesaurus.

Varying Voices

Isabella was listening to the radio and scribbling notes down in a book.

"What on earth are you doing?" asked Max.

"I'm collecting voices for my story, Max," she said. "I just heard an interview with a writer who says that what people say, and how they say it, tells us a lot about them, and she says the same is true for the characters in our stories. The trouble is, I think it would be really boring to have to keep describing people's voices. I wish there was a quicker way."

"There is, Izzy," replied Max. "**Adverbs** add extra information about **verbs**, to help your reader get a better idea of what is going on. They are a brilliant way to tell your reader more about how your characters are talking."

"I see," said Isabella. "So I could say, *'Go away,' said Ben, rudely.*"

"Exactly," Max replied. "Adverbs help to let your reader know what kind of person your character is, and how they are feeling at that moment. So a bully might talk *spitefully*, but the person he is bullying might talk *timidly*."

"Wow, I see what you mean. That's a great trick," said Isabella.

"Ah, but there's more! You can do an even better job by teaming up your adverbs with really strong verbs. Using *said* all the time is really boring. Try *stammered nervously*, *mumbled shyly*, or *grunted gruffly* instead," suggested Max.

"Thanks Max. Who would have thought there are so many ways to speak?" said Isabella.

Put words in their mouths!

Look at the line-up of characters below and read the description of how each of them speaks. Draw a line to join each character up with the best speech bubble for them.

snaps gruffly

whispers shyly

asks cheerfully

snaps rudely

enquires politely

What are you staring at?

Please can I play?

Could you tell me the time?

Do you want to feed him?

Where's the money?

Top Tips!

Don't forget to pay attention to the actual words your characters are saying. If you want them to be happy or angry, what they say has to reflect that.

Did you know?

You can use two adverbs together for extra power. *Very* is a particularly useful one for this. *"I'm scared," she whispered, very quietly.*

Secrets and Lies

It was Sir Ralph Witherbottom's birthday the next day, and Isabella had hidden a surprise for him in her bedroom.

"I need you to help me keep it a secret, Max. You mustn't tell him where it is!" said Isabella.

"But what if he asks?" pondered Max.

"Just say the opposite of where it really is, so he won't know where to look," suggested Isabella.

"Ah, **antonyms**. Now you're talking," replied Max.

"Am I?" asked Isabella. "What on earth are antonyms?"

"They are words with opposite meanings," explained Max. "Like *full* and *empty*. They are quite interesting, really. You see, lots of words have one antonym, like *high* and *low,* for example. But some words have more than one antonym, like *short*, for example. *Long* and *tall* are both antonyms for *short*. That's because there is more than one way something can be short."

"Well that's all very interesting, Max, but what are they for?" she asked.

"Well, antonyms tend to be **adjectives** or **adverbs**, which makes them really useful for describing and comparing things," pointed out Max. "So you can have a *hot* drink or a *cold* drink, and you can walk *quickly* or *slowly*. Using two antonyms together can be very effective. Writing about going from daylight into a dark cave, for example, can really help to paint a picture."

"Spooky stuff!" laughed Isabella.

Where's the present?

Here's a coded note explaining where a hoard of Christmas presents is hidden. Use an antonym of each underlined word to discover where the presents really are, then write the true words in the spaces.

The Christmas presents are hidden <u>outside</u> ______________ the locked box in the spare room.

I have put the box <u>above</u> ______________ the bed, in the <u>left</u> ______________ hand corner.

The key is hidden on the <u>top</u> ______________ shelf of the bookshelf, behind the <u>smallest</u> ______________ book.

We'll put the presents under the Christmas tree <u>before</u> ______________ the children come <u>up</u> ______________ to breakfast tomorrow.

Top Tips!

Try using the **suffixes** *ful* and *less* for making antonyms.

careful *careless*

fearful *fearless*

Did you know?

It isn't just suffixes that can create antonyms – lots of **prefixes** can, too.

legal	➔	*illegal*	*fiction*	➔	*non-fiction*
usual	➔	*unusual*	*understand*	➔	*misunderstand*
polite	➔	*impolite*	*accurate*	➔	*inaccurate*
regular	➔	*irregular*			

Revise Time

1 Think of a synonym for each of these words.

a happy __________

b ill __________

c spooky __________

d old __________

e mend __________

f laugh __________

2 Finish these sentences by using an adverb to describe how you think each character might speak.

a The colonel shouted __________ at the soldiers.

b The baby gurgled __________ in its pram.

c The mums chatted __________ about the new school.

d The policeman spoke __________ to the lost girl.

e The boys argued __________ about the rules.

f Katie whispered __________ in the darkness.

3 Draw lines to match up these words with their antonyms.

a cold	old
b young	dirty
c dry	hate
d useful	hot
e clean	useless
f love	wet

4 Choose a suitable synonym to replace the word in brackets in each of these sentences.

a We have just moved into our new (home). ____________________

b My little sister is upstairs having a (sleep). ____________________

c We (discovered) a cave on the beach. ____________________

d We ordered a (big) pizza. ____________________

e The old house was really (creepy). ____________________

f My homework is really (tricky). ____________________

5 Underline the adverbs in these sentences.

a The teacher explained the task carefully to the children.

b Michael laughed loudly at Ben's joke.

c The girl shouted angrily.

d The boy spoke reassuringly to the injured animal.

e The squirrel scampered swiftly up the tree.

f Beth tore the paper off her present excitedly.

6 Complete these sentences by finding the antonyms of the words in brackets.

a We thought the boat would (float) ____________________.

b Grandad was (awake) ____________________ when we arrived.

c Mum helped me (do) ____________________ my zip.

d I knew I was going to (lose) ____________________ the chess game.

e My Dad has a lovely (new) ____________________ car.

f The kite flew (low) ____________________ over the trees.

Fair Play

Isabella was not happy. She'd just come back from a long tennis lesson and now she had to face her homework.

"Can you help me, Max?" she pleaded. "I'm in a muddle trying to get my characters to talk to each other. I can never remember how to set out their **dialogue** on the page."

"OK, well I suppose it's a bit like a tennis match," explained Max. "When two of your characters are talking, it's like a ball going backwards and forwards over the net – one character says something, and the other replies. You need to separate what each character says, so that every time someone new starts to talk, you start on a new line."

"It can't be that simple, Max," said Isabella.

"Well, not quite," admitted Max. "You have to use **speech marks**, so your readers know that one of the characters is speaking. They go at the start, and the end, of each section of dialogue."

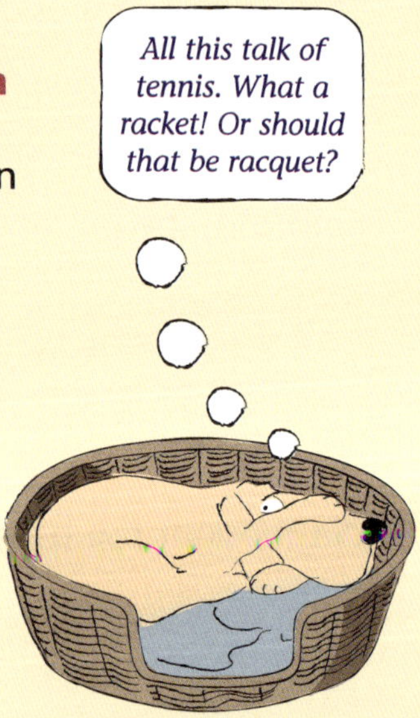

"And what about the **commas**?" asked Isabella.

"Well, if the dialogue starts in the middle of a sentence," explained Max, "you put the comma *before* you open the speech marks. So you would write *Max said, 'Your room is a mess.'* If you start your sentence with dialogue, however, the comma goes just inside the speech marks at the *end* of the dialogue, for instance, *"Your room is a mess," said Max."*

"Brilliant, Max," exclaimed a delighted Isabella. "With your help, it'll be game, set and match to Isabella when I write my story!"

Be the umpire

Dialogue is all about taking turns, but one of these characters isn't getting a word in edgeways. Make things fairer by writing in some dialogue for him.

Top Tips

You don't always have to say their name each time a character replies, but you must make sure that it's clear who's speaking at all times.

Did you know?

Dialogue is also called **direct speech**. If you report what a character said, but not in their actual words, this is called **reported** or **indirect speech**, for instance, *Emma said goodbye.*

Sentences with Style

Isabella was writing a letter to her new pen pal.

"She is so stylish, Max," she said admiringly. "She lives in Paris and has so many great clothes – *and* she writes well. My letter just makes me sound like a baby!"

"Why not try combining some of those simple sentences into longer ones? If you use the right punctuation, your sentences will flow beautifully."

"Good idea, Max," said Isabella, "but where do I start?"

"Well," said Max, "**compound sentences** are like two **simple sentences** joined together, and they often need a **comma** to join the two **clauses** together. So you might write *I love clothes, so I went shopping.*

"**Complex sentences** often have a **main clause** and a **subordinate clause** and again, you often need a comma between them," he went on. "The really complicated ones have an **embedded clause** in the middle, and then you really do need commas. So you could write *My new top, with the sparkly straps, is really gorgeous.*"

"Are commas the only thing you can use, Max?" asked Isabella.

"No," he replied. "You can use **semi-colons** in compound sentences, if you need a slightly longer pause, and if the second clause in your sentence gives you extra information about the first, you can use a **colon**. So you could write *I need to go shopping: I have nothing to wear.*"

"How did you know, Max? Are you offering to take me shopping?" she laughed. "Thanks!"

Best-dressed sentences

Mix and match these sentences by choosing an ending for each of these sentence openings.

1 He was cold:

2 The car, which was very old,

3 It was hot,

4 My cousin,

5 Although we were late,

we saw most of the film.

who is 24 years old, is getting married.

it was snowing.

so we bought a cold drink.

ground to a halt.

Top Tips!

If you read a compound or complex sentence out loud and you need to pause, that's where you need a comma.

Did you know?

Commas aren't the only way to join clauses together. You can use **connectives** like *so*, *and* or *but* as well, and often you will need both. Read your sentences carefully to make sure you have connected your clauses together properly, so the whole sentence makes sense.

Building Texts

Max and Isabella were building Spotless a new kennel from a flat-pack kit.

"You make DIY look easy, Max," said Isabella. "Are you any good at putting bits of text together too? We've been learning about **connectives** at school. I think they are words or phrases you can use to link together **clauses** in a sentence."

"That's right, Izzy," he replied. "You can use them to join sentences or paragraphs together, too. They can even help to join chapters together."

"But how do they work?" she asked.

"Well, with glue and nails, these planks of wood will become a kennel. It's the same with bits of text," explained Max. "Connectives can link them together into something that really makes sense. Connectives like *and* and *also* let you add one idea to another. *But* and *however* let you oppose ideas, and *because*, *so* and *this means* allow you to show that one thing is caused by another. You can also use connectives like *just then* or *after that* to show when things happened."

"I see, Max. So you could write – *Spotless just kept eating, so he got really fat. In the end we had to buy him a bigger kennel,"* laughed Isabella.

"That's right. The word *so* in the first sentence links the two clauses together, and *'In the end'* at the start of the next sentence joins the two sentences together," he explained.

"Just like glue, Max. You've solved another sticky situation!" declared Isabella.

Build a kennel

Choose the best plank of wood to fill each of the gaps in the kennel. Use the shape of the planks to help you decide.

Top Tips!

Then is used far too much as a connective. Try to think of better ones to use instead. Try *suddenly*, *just after that*, or *almost immediately*.

Did you know?

Changing a connective can completely alter the meaning of a sentence.

She was happy because they moved house.
She was happy until they moved house.

Revise Time

1 Add the speech punctuation to these sentences.

a Sit down ordered Mr Hayes.

b Julie asked Is it my turn?

c I'll be back soon said Dad.

d Can I play asked Chloe.

e You can leave your bag here explained the teacher.

f Jamie shouted That's mine!

2 Underline the embedded clause in these sentences.

a The cat, which was black, was fast asleep.

b It was cold, and wet, so we took the car.

c Last Saturday, in the evening, we went to the cinema.

d Sally, my big sister, can play the piano.

e Mrs Rogers, from next door, took care of our rabbit.

f My dog, Bouncer, can do tricks.

3 Sort these connectives into the three boxes, according to their meaning.

however   this means   as a result   also

in addition to   nevertheless

as well as	but	and because

4 Circle the sentences that are punctuated incorrectly.

a "I'm tired!" grumbled Ava.

b Let's go shopping," suggested Mum.

c "Can I have another cake? pleaded Max."

d Amy asked, "Have you seen my shoes?"

e Paul argued, It's my turn now.

f Daniel yawned, "I'm so tired!"

5 Add the commas to these sentences.

a Mr Painter my teacher loves to read.

b Vanilla ice cream with chocolate sauce is my favourite.

c The water which was cold dripped down my neck.

d Jack my best friend is moving house.

e We watched the postman on his bike coming down the road.

f The chocolate which had melted in the wrapper oozed out all over me.

6 Underline the connectives in these sentences.

a I found my trainers then went to play football.

b I took an apple because I was hungry.

c I put sunscreen on so I wouldn't burn.

d We ran as fast as we could but we still missed the bus.

e However much water I drank, I still felt thirsty.

f Despite the rain, we had a great day out.

The Whole Truth?

"Max, I think I've finished my homework, so can I go out now?" asked Isabella.

"What do you mean you *think* you've finished?" queried Max.

"Well, I thought I'd written down what the teacher said we should do, but my friend Rebecca says there is another section to do as well, which I must have missed," said Isabella.

"Well, what was the homework about, anyway?" he asked.

"Our teacher asked us to find out about **direct** and **reported speech**," she replied.

"Oh, that's easy," said Max. "Direct speech is also called **dialogue**. It's when you write the exact words that a character says. So if you had written exactly what your teacher had said, for instance, that would have been direct speech," said Max, pointedly. "With direct speech, you need to use **speech marks**, so your reader knows that someone is speaking."

"Oh, yes, I remember now," said Isabella. "What about reported speech, then?"

"Well, that's when you report what someone has said, but not in their actual words. A bit like what you wrote down about your homework. You don't need speech marks for that," explained Max.

"So why have two different types of speech, then?" asked Isabella.

"Well," went on Max, "direct speech is useful because it helps to bring your characters to life, but too much of it can be hard to read, especially if you keep swapping between characters.

"Reported speech doesn't always reveal as much about your characters, but it can help you to cover a lot of story quite quickly, by summing up what different people say. It also means you can include what a character says without them actually having to be there in the story.

"Most good stories use a mix of the two," explained Max, "but the big lesson for you, Izzy, is to always include all the important information, whatever type you choose!"

Complete the cartoon

Read the direct and reported speech in this passage and use it to help you fill in the speech bubbles in the cartoon.

Dad said that it was time to pack up the car.
"Then we are ready to go," said Mum.

"Are we nearly there?" asked Milly.
Tom said that he felt sick.

Tom said he was going to play in the sea.
"This is fun!" exclaimed Milly.

Both children said that they didn't want to go home.

Top Tips

If you have to write a lot of direct speech, try breaking it up with a passage of reported speech. It can be easier to read and varies the pace of your writing.

Did you know?

Newspaper journalists like to use direct quotes from people in their articles, because it's more interesting to read the actual words that someone has said. It can sometimes sound more believable than reported speech, too.

Where is it?

Isabella phoned Max one lunchtime, from school.

"Max, could you bring my homework book into school, please? I've forgotten it again. It's on my desk," she explained.

Max ran upstairs to have a look, and came back out of breath.

"Sorry Izzy. It's not there," he panted.

"Try on my bed, then," she suggested.

Max puffed his way back up the stairs again, and back down again. "Not there," he said breathlessly. "What homework do you need, anyway?"

"It's the **preposition** worksheet I did last night," explained Isabella.

"Ah yes, I remember. You could do with some more accurate prepositions now, to help me find your book. Prepositions are words that describe the relationship between two **nouns**, **pronouns**, or a noun and a pronoun."

He went on, "They are particularly good at describing where things are, like *on*, *under* or *in*. So you could write – *He is* ***in*** *the garden*. But you might also write – *I bought the book* ***for*** *you*. We'd be lost without prepositions, a bit like your book!"

"Very funny, Max," scoffed Isabella.

"No seriously, they are pretty important, because they change the meaning of a sentence completely. So looking *on* your bed would be a waste of time if the book was *under* your bed, wouldn't it?" said Max.

"Oh dear," said Isabella sheepishly, at the other end of the phone. "It's not just the preposition that was wrong, but the noun too. I've just found the book, *in* my bag. Sorry!"

Tidy that room!

Look closely at this picture of Claire's bedroom. Messy isn't it? Choose the best preposition to complete these sentences.

1 Claire's boots are ______________________ her bed.

2 Her school bag is ______________________ the desk and the wardrobe.

3 She has left her pencil case ______________________ the rug.

4 Her hockey stick is ______________________ her desk.

5 Her jacket is ______________________ the back of her chair.

6 Her hairbrush is ______________________ the cupboard.

Top Tips!

Match your prepositions to the kind of writing you are doing. *Upon* and *beneath* sound much more formal than *on* and *under*.

Did you know?

Children used to be taught never to put a preposition at the end of a sentence. Thankfully that rule doesn't apply much now, because it led to some very awkward sentences!

What are you looking at? *At what are you looking?*

High Standards

Isabella was in disgrace. She had left a terrible mess in the bathroom again. To make amends, she tidied it beautifully and promised not to do it again.

"Good girl, Izzy," said Sir Ralph. "You see, if we all agree to stick to the rules then we know where we are."

"You sound like this literacy book, Dad," laughed Isabella. "It says here that **nouns** and **verbs** should agree, too. What does that mean?"

"Oh, that's simple enough," he said. "It just means that you need to choose the right form of a verb to match the noun you are writing about. So you would write *a dog scratches* but ***two** dogs scratch*. Noun and verb agreement is an important part of something called standard English. That just means the rules we follow when we are writing, so our readers can understand us."

"What other rules are there, then?" asked Isabella.

"Well, another important rule helps us to write about negatives. You must only ever use one negative word in a sentence. So you could write *I never eat eggs*, or *I don't ever eat eggs*, but you wouldn't write *I don't never eat eggs*," said Sir Ralph.

"Follow those rules, Izzy, and we'll all get along fine!" laughed Sir Ralph.

Find those rule-breakers

Circle the places in these newspaper cuttings where the rules of standard English have been broken.

CRISIS AT VICARAGE

The vicar has said that if his cat escape again he won't never get over it. The cat jump over the wall every time the vicar open the door.

There is a reward for anyone who phone with information.

JUST FOR FUN

A dozen boys from the high school will take part in the fun run on Wednesday. They sets off at 11am from the village green on the five mile course. PE teacher Mr Speedy say, "The boys haven't never run this far before, so we will have to see how they does."

big
so w
he
kill
fron
chic
big
sock
snov
is
ther
cho
Mar
low
now

Top Tips!

As well as noun and verb agreement, there are rules about the *kinds* of words you should use. Unless you are writing very informally, or writing dialogue for a character, you should avoid unusual conversational words when you are writing.

Did you know?

Most of the time we try to write standard English, but the way we speak might be quite different. Depending on our backgrounds, we speak with different dialects – that means differences in grammar and vocabulary. Standard English is just one dialect, but even that changes over time.

Revise Time

1 Decide whether each of these sentences is direct or reported speech. Tick the right box when you have made up your mind.

		direct speech	reported speech
a	Rob said he would come round later.	☐	☐
b	"Where is my tennis racquet?" asked Sam.	☐	☐
c	"I'm hungry!" complained Max.	☐	☐
d	Serena asked if she could watch TV.	☐	☐
e	Raj asked, "What time is it?"	☐	☐
f	Dad said he was going to a football match.	☐	☐

2 Underline the prepositions in these sentences.

a The cat jumped onto the fence.

b Jo peeped through the keyhole.

c Jay dropped the rubbish into the bin.

d The duck took the bread from my fingers.

e We sheltered under a tree.

f Peter passed the salt across the table.

3 Choose the correct form of the verb to match the nouns.

a David (laugh / laughs) ____________________

b I (swims / swim) ____________________

c We (play / plays) ____________________

d They (wash / washes) ____________________

e You (sleep / sleeps) ____________________

f It (watches / watch) ____________________

4 **Rewrite these sentences as reported speech.**

a "That's my game!" snapped Jacob.

b "It's not fair," complained Rory.

c "Happy birthday!" cheered the class.

d Our teacher said, "It's time to go out to play."

e Mum asked, "Have you tidied your room yet, Matthew?"

f Sally giggled, "Dad looks daft in that hat!"

5 **Write a sentence linking each pair of nouns. Choose a preposition from the box to link the nouns.**

outside under against into onto behind

a dog fence

b car garage

c book floor

d pizza oven

e key sofa

f ball wall

6 **In some of these sentences, the nouns and verbs do not agree. Underline where this happens.**

a Louise jump really high when we do high jump.

b Paul and I look great in our new ski suits.

c My baby sister cry all night.

d Heather and Claire try to stop squabbling.

e We eats our packed lunch in the dining hall.

f I love chocolate.

Made from Memories

Max was showing Isabella some photos taken when he was a little boy.

"This was taken on holiday in Cornwall," he reminisced. "We had an adventure that year. We went out fishing in a little boat and had to be rescued by a lifeboat. I wrote a **recount** of it later and won a prize at school. Those were the days!"

"A recount? What's that?" asked Isabella.

"A recount is where you re-tell events in the order in which they happened, so that someone who wasn't there can understand them," Max explained. "You don't have to include every tiny detail, but all the important facts need to be there. Recounts are sometimes called **chronological reports**."

"Do you need to use any special words?" she said.

"Well, recounts are written in the past tense, because they are describing events that have already happened. You link the events together using time **connectives** like *after that*, *suddenly*, and *immediately*," he explained.

"You also have to describe things quite carefully, so your choice of **adverbs** and **adjectives** is very important. And remember, a recount is about what actually happened, not about how you felt about it all. Stick to the facts," he advised.

To the rescue!

These pictures of a sea rescue were taken by the coastguard. Help the coastguard use them to write a recount. Number the boxes 1 to 5 so they are sorted into chronological order.

Top Tips!

Time connectives like *earlier*, *later* and *before* are very important in recounts, but try not to use *then* too often. It gets really boring!

Did you know?

You can write **non-chronological** reports too. They are information texts that are structured around topics rather than time order.

Taking the Best Bits

Sir Ralph Witherbottom was busy in his study, working his way through a thick science magazine.

"What on earth are you doing, Dad?" asked Isabella. "You've been in here for ages!"

"Well, it's a thick issue this time. I'm taking notes from the best articles, so when I read them again next time, it won't take so long," replied Sir Ralph.

"How do you take notes, Dad?" she asked.

"Well, taking notes is all about picking the most important bits of information from a text, so you can use them later, or for someone else to look at," explained Sir Ralph. "You have to **skim** through the text first, so you understand the general meaning, and then you **scan** it again looking for key facts and figures, and any useful headings.

"Underlining words can save you time, and you can make notes in the margin too. But you must keep your handwriting neat so you can read it later, and that's not always easy if you are writing quickly," he added.

"What if you're taking notes from something that someone is saying?" wondered Isabella.

"Well that's harder to do, because there's no text to write on, and you can't look back if you need to. You have to decide straight away if each bit of information is important. Don't try to write down every word the person says, or you'll never manage," advised Sir Ralph.

"You make it sound easy. But the question is, are your notes as boring as the original?" asked Isabella, laughing.

Guess the book

If you have taken good notes, other people should be able to understand them. Read each set of notes, decide what kind of book it might come from, then draw the cover of the book and give it a title.

Battle of Hastings	Australia	1969, moon landing
1066	Southern hemisphere	First man on moon: Neil Armstrong
William the Conqueror	Capital city: Sydney	"One small step for man, one giant leap for mankind."
Norman Conquest	Wildlife: kangaroos, koala bears	

Top Tips!

Read your notes through soon after you have finished, to make sure they make sense. If you leave it until later, you may not remember enough to fill in any gaps.

Did you know?

Journalists learn shorthand, which is a special written language developed especially for noting lots of information very quickly when people are speaking.

The Art of Persuasion

Isabella was hoping to go to the theatre with a friend. The only trouble was, it would mean a late night and there was school the next day.

"There must be *some* way of persuading Dad, Max. What would *you* say?" asked Isabella, hopefully.

"Persuasion is all about getting someone to see your point of view," said Max.

"It's the same with persuasive writing," he went on. "You have to focus on the benefits, not on the drawbacks. So you should say that a trip to the theatre would be educational for you, and that the play is one you are studying next year. Remind him that he has been saying for ages how you should go out somewhere with Beth, and that he loves the theatre himself, so surely he must understand why you want to go."

"But will that be enough to persuade him?" wondered Isabella. "He's going to worry about the late night."

"Well, you need to tackle that head-on. So you can say you know it will mean a late night, but you can go to bed early the night before and you have a quiet day at school the day afterwards anyway. Think of any objections he might have, and come up with an answer," suggested Max.

"You'll have him wrapped around your finger in no time!" he laughed.

Be persuasive!

Imagine you are trying to persuade your dad to buy you a new bike. What would you say, and how would your dad respond?

You: Dad, can I have a new bike?

Dad: I'm not sure. You haven't had your bike for that long, and new ones are very expensive. Why do you need a new one?

You:

Dad:

You:

Dad:

Top Tips!

You can use these persuasive techniques for writing really effective adverts.

Did you know?

Thinking ahead about any objections to your point of view makes it much harder for anyone to disagree with you. Just be careful not to include too many of these objections, or people will spot that there are loads of potential problems with your idea. Make sure you list more benefits than possible objections.

Revise Time

1 Underline the time connectives in this recount.

I was in the park last week when a boy on a bike whizzed past me, knocking me over. Once he had seen what he'd done, he sped off, leaving me on the ground. After I got home and told Mum, she took me to the hospital immediately. At the hospital, the doctor took an X-ray of my ankle before saying it was sprained. After that, he put a bandage on it and eventually we went home.

2 Use your skimming and scanning skills to find the facts in this piece of text that you need to answer the questions. Underline the key pieces of information as you work through the text.

Gran was born in 1936 in London. When the war broke out, the Germans dropped bombs on London so Gran was evacuated to Wales with her brothers James and Eddie. They stayed on a farm there, and Gran remembers milking the goats.

Gran can remember when rationing ended, and having a banana for the first time.

a When was the writer's grandmother born? ____________________

b Where was she born? ____________________

c Where was she evacuated? ____________________

d Why? ____________________

e What were her brothers' names? ____________________

f What animal did Gran milk? ____________________

3 A supermarket wants to build a new store in your town. Here are some of the arguments in favour of the new shop. Think of three arguments against the new store.

For

- The new supermarket will mean that people don't have to travel so far to do their shopping.
- It will provide new jobs for people in the town.
- It will offer people a better range of cheaper foods than other local shops.

Against

1 ____

2 ____

3 ____

4 Rewrite this text as a recount of what happened to Courtney.

Courtney stopped walking at midday for lunch. She had got up at dawn that morning to make sandwiches for her journey, and stopped in the high street at ten o'clock to buy some lemonade. After lunch she would walk to the bus stop and wait for the one o'clock bus.

5 Write a time line of the American War of Independence. Use your scanning skills to pick out the dates you need from this piece of writing.

Until 1775, the 13 colonies of British North America were governed from London. The colonies had no right to vote, but they still had to pay taxes, and when Parliament raised taxes again, they rebelled.

The first shots of the war were fired in April 1775 when British soldiers tried to destroy weapons held by the colonists at Boston. Fighting was fierce and in March 1776, the British fled from Boston.

On 4 July 1776, the Declaration of Independence was adopted by all 13 colonies.

6 Here are three arguments against a suggestion to scrap school uniform. Think of three arguments in favour of the idea.

Against

- School uniform helps children to feel they belong to a school.
- Children may feel under pressure to buy and wear the latest fashions.
- Parents will have to spend a lot more money on clothing for children to wear to school.

For

1 ______

2 ______

3 ______

Glossary

adjective a word or phrase added to a noun to add to or modify it

adverb a word or phrase that adds to or modifies a verb, e.g. run quickly, very tired

antonyms words with opposite meanings, e.g. big, small

chronological report a report of events in the order in which they happened. Also called recount

clause a distinct part of a sentence.
The main clause is the main part of the sentence. It makes sense on its own.
The subordinate clause adds extra information but does not make sense on its own.
An embedded clause is placed in the middle of a sentence

colon (:) a punctuation mark used to introduce a list or quotation, or to separate clauses in a sentence

comma (,) a punctuation mark that shows when to pause, separates clauses or items in a list

complex sentences sentences that contain a main clause and a subordinate clause

compound sentences sentences where two equally weighted clauses are joined together with a conjunction

connective a word or phrase used to connect different parts of a text, e.g. because, but, later

consonant all the letters of the alphabet except the vowels a, e, i, o and u

dialogue words spoken by characters in a story. Also called direct speech

direct speech words actually spoken, enclosed in speech marks

embedded clause a clause that is placed in the middle of a sentence, enclosed by commas

indirect speech when something someone says is reported, but not using their actual words. Also called reported speech

main clause the main clause in a sentence. It makes sense on its own

mnemonic a memorable phrase that helps you remember spelling patterns

non-chronological report a report whose structure is based on topics rather than the order of events

noun a word that names a thing or feeling

plural more than one of something. Usually made by adding s, es, or ies, e.g. cars, bushes, babies. There are some exceptions, e.g. people, children

prefix a group of letters added to the beginning of a word to change its meaning, e.g. unhappy, disobedient

preposition a word that describes the relationship between two nouns, two pronouns or a noun and a pronoun, e.g. in, on, under, for

pronoun a word used instead of a noun, to avoid using the same noun again

pronounce to say a word or a sound in a certain way

recount a chronological report

reported speech when something someone says is reported, but not using their actual words. Also called indirect speech

scan to read quickly to find a specific piece of information

semi-colon (;) a punctuation mark used to separate phrases or clauses in a sentence. Stronger than a comma but not as strong as a full stop

simple sentence a sentence with a single clause

singular one of something, e.g. a dog, the girl

skim to read quickly to understand the main meaning of a text

speech marks ("") punctuation marks used to indicate direct speech

subordinate clause in a complex sentence, the subordinate clause adds extra information but does not make sense on its own

suffix a group of letters added to the end of a root word to change its meaning, e.g. helpless, boldly

synonyms words with the same or similar meaning, e.g. cold, chilly

verb a doing or being word

vowel a, e, i, o and u. The other letters in the alphabet are consonants

Answers

Page 5

3 balloons, 2 boxes, 4 lollies, 2 toy cats, 4 watches, 2 keys

Page 7

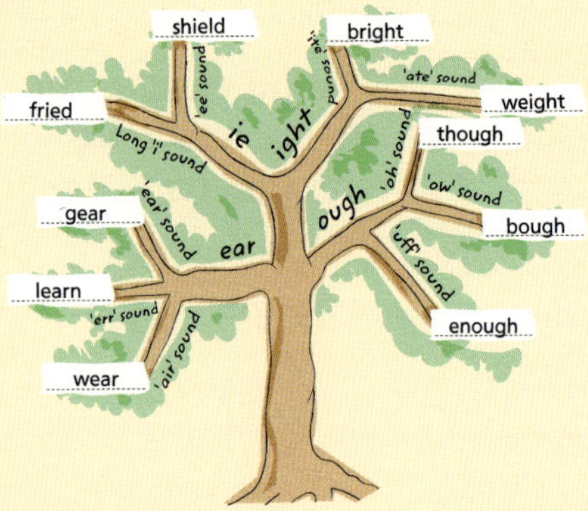

Page 9

The incorrectly spelt words are: makeing, lifless, shamful, brokeen

Pages 10–11 Revision exercises

Exercise 1

a house – houses
b worry – worries
c fox – foxes
d girl – girls
e chair – chairs
f ruby – rubies

Exercise 2

a lie, tie
b thought, sought
c hook, look
d fear, near
e pour, your
f niece, piece

Exercise 3

a loving
b surely
c tuneless
d nicer
e tuneful
f braver

Exercise 4

a dishes
b patches
c balls
d cities
e houses
f children

Exercise 5

a ear: heard, near
b ie: relief, tie
c ight: bright, height

Exercise 6

a saving
b ageless
c usable
d careful
e sharing
f biggest

Page 13

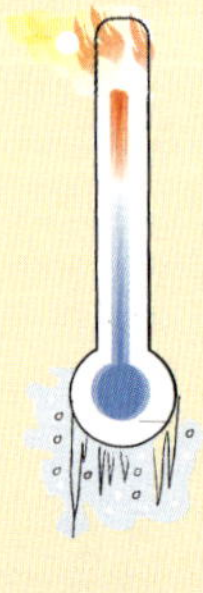

boiling
hot
warm
tepid
cool
chilly
cold
freezing

Page 15

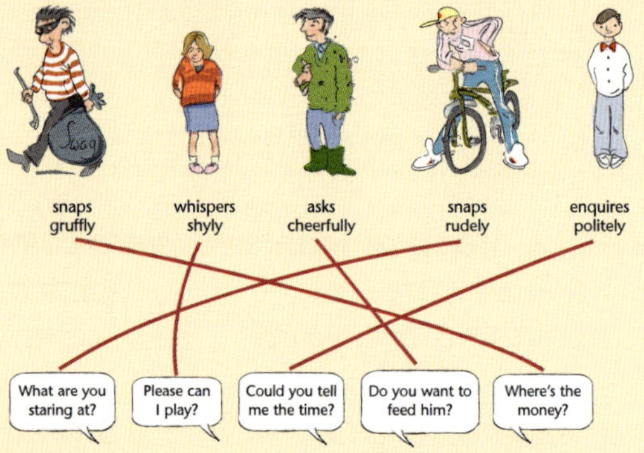

Page 17

The Christmas presents are hidden inside the locked box in the spare room.

I have put the box under the bed, in the right hand corner.

The key is hidden on the bottom shelf of the bookshelf, behind the biggest book.

We'll put the presents under the Christmas tree after the children come down to breakfast tomorrow.

Pages 18–19 Revision exercises

Exercise 1

Synonyms will vary, but appropriate ones include:

a happy, cheerful
b ill, sick
c spooky, creepy
d old, ancient
e mend, fix
f laugh, giggle

Exercise 2

Adverbs chosen will vary, but appropriate ones include:

a The colonel shouted loudly at the soldiers.
b The baby gurgled happily in its pram.
c The mums chatted cheerfully about the new school.
d The policeman spoke gently to the lost girl.
e The boys argued crossly about the rules.
f Kate whispered quietly in the darkness.

Exercise 3

a cold – hot
b young – old
c dry – wet
d useful – useless
e clean – dirty
f love – hate

Exercise 4

Synonyms chosen will vary, but appropriate ones include:

a We have just moved into our new house.
b My little sister is upstairs having a nap.
c We found a cave on the beach.
d We ordered a large pizza.
e The old house was really scary.
f My homework is really hard.

Exercise 5

- **a** The teacher explained the task carefully to the children.
- **b** Michael laughed loudly at Ben's joke.
- **c** The girl shouted angrily.
- **d** The boy spoke reassuringly to the injured animal.
- **e** The squirrel scampered swiftly up the tree.
- **f** Beth tore the paper off her present excitedly.

Exercise 6

- **a** We thought the boat would sink.
- **b** Grandad was asleep when we arrived.
- **c** Mum helped me to undo my zip.
- **d** I knew I was going to win the chess game.
- **e** My Dad has a lovely old car.
- **f** The kite flew high over the trees.

Page 21

Dialogue will vary, but should be set out using correct punctuation, and each section should form an appropriate reply to the previous one.

Page 23

1. He was cold: it was snowing.
2. The car, which was very old, ground to a halt.
3. It was hot, so we bought a cold drink.
4. My cousin, who is 24 years old, is getting married.
5. Although we were late, we saw most of the film.

Page 25

Pages 26–27 Revision exercises

Exercise 1

- **a** "Sit down!" ordered Mr Hayes.
- **b** Julie asked, "Is it my turn?"
- **c** "I'll be back soon," said Dad.
- **d** "Can I play?" asked Chloe.
- **e** "You can leave your bag here," explained the teacher.
- **f** Jamie shouted, "That's mine!"

Exercise 2

- **a** The cat, which was black, was fast asleep.
- **b** It was cold, and wet, so we took the car.
- **c** Last Saturday, in the evening, we went to the cinema.
- **d** Sally, my big sister, can play the piano.
- **e** Mrs Rogers, from next door, took care of our rabbit.
- **f** My dog, Bouncer, can do tricks.

Exercise 3

as well as: also, in addition to
but: however, nevertheless
and because: this means, as a result

Exercise 4

The incorrectly punctuated sentences are **b**, **c** and **e**.

Exercise 5

- **a** Mr Painter, my teacher, loves to read.
- **b** Vanilla ice cream, with chocolate sauce, is my favourite.
- **c** The water, which was cold, dripped down my neck.
- **d** Jack, my best friend, is moving house.
- **e** We watched the postman, on his bike, coming down the road.
- **f** The chocolate, which had melted in the wrapper, oozed out all over me.

Exercise 6

- **a** I found my trainers then went to play football.
- **b** I took an apple because I was hungry.
- **c** I put sunscreen on so I wouldn't burn.
- **d** We ran as fast as we could but we still missed the bus.
- **e** However much water I drank, I still felt thirsty.
- **f** Despite the rain, we had a great day out.

Page 29

Page 31

1. Claire's boots are under her bed.
2. Her school bag is between the desk and the wardrobe.
3. She has left her pencil case on the rug.
4. Her hockey stick is behind the desk.
5. Her jacket is on the back of her chair.
6. Her hairbrush is in the cupboard.

Page 33

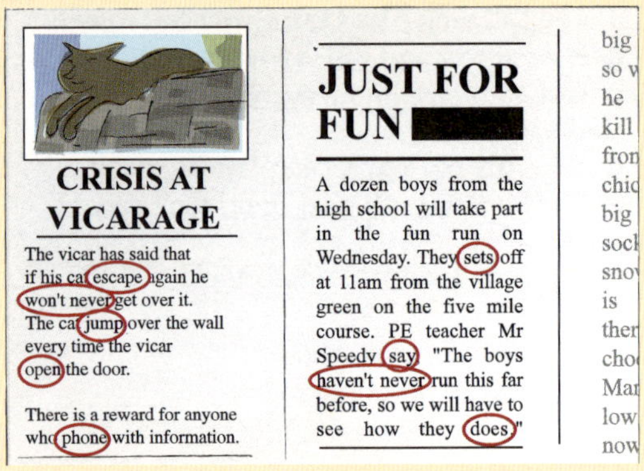

CRISIS AT VICARAGE

The vicar has said that if his cat escape again he won't never get over it. The cat jump over the wall every time the vicar open the door.

There is a reward for anyone who phone with information.

JUST FOR FUN

A dozen boys from the high school will take part in the fun run on Wednesday. They sets off at 11am from the village green on the five mile course. PE teacher Mr Speedy say, "The boys haven't never run this far before, so we will have to see how they does."

big
so w
he
kill
fron
chic
big
sock
sno
is
ther
cho
Mar
low
now

Pages 34–35 Revision exercises

Exercise 1

Direct speech: **b**, **c** and **e**

Reported speech: **a**, **d** and **f**

Exercise 2

a The cat jumped <u>onto</u> the fence.
b Jo peeped <u>through</u> the keyhole.
c Jay dropped the rubbish <u>into</u> the bin.
d The duck took the bread <u>from</u> my fingers.
e We sheltered <u>under</u> a tree.
f Peter passed the salt <u>across</u> the table.

Exercise 3

a David laughs
b I swim
c We play
d They wash
e You sleep
f It watches

Exercise 4

a Jacob snapped that it was his game.
b Rory complained that it was not fair.
c The class all cheered happy birthday.
d Our teacher said it was time to go out and play.
e Mum asked if Matthew had tidied his room yet.
f Sally giggled that Dad looked daft in his hat.

Exercise 5

Sentences will vary, but each should include both nouns and one of the prepositions.

Exercise 6

The nouns and verbs in these sentences do not agree.

a Louise <u>jump</u> really high when we do high jump.
c My baby sister <u>cry</u> all night.
e We <u>eats</u> our packed lunch in the dining hall.

Page 37

Page 39

Book covers will vary, but should be appropriate to the notes given for each book.

Page 41

Persuasive texts will vary, but good ones will counter each objection to buying a new bike with a well constructed argument. Strong texts may also anticipate Dad's objections.

Pages 42–43 Revision exercises

Exercise 1

I was in the park last week <u>when</u> a boy on a bike whizzed past me, knocking me over. <u>Once</u> he had seen what he'd done, he sped off, leaving me on the ground. <u>After</u> I got home and told Mum, she took me to the hospital immediately. At the hospital, the doctor took an X-ray of my ankle <u>before</u> saying it was sprained. <u>After that</u>, he put a bandage on it and <u>eventually</u> we went home.

Exercise 2

a 1936
b London
c Wales
d Because the Germans bombed London.
e James and Eddie
f goats

Exercise 3

Objections to the supermarket will vary, but might include reference to other local shops already in business, noisy and disruptive building work, effect on the environment, increased traffic etc.

Exercise 4

Recounts will vary, but should describe Courtney's day in chronological order.

Exercise 5

1775
Parliament raises taxes
April 1775
First shots of war fired near Boston
March 1776
British flee Boston
4 July 1776
Declaration of Independence adopted

Exercise 6

Arguments given will vary, but might include the fact that children do not like wearing school uniform and find it unfashionable. Parents would not have to spend money on uniform, and children could express their personalities in the clothes they wore.